The Standard Publishing Company, Cincinnati, Ohio.
A division of Standex International Corporation.
© 1992 by The Standard Publishing Company
Printed in the United States of America
99 98 97 96 95 94 93 92   5 4 3 2 1

Library of Congress Cataloging-in-Publication Data
Faltico, Mary Lou.
Song of the seed / based on the song by Cecile Lamb
and Mildred Adair Stagg: illustrated by Mary Lou Faltico.
ISBN 0-87403-956-8
Library of Congress Catalog Card Number 91-46806

Song of the Seed

Based on the song by
**Cecile Lamb and
Mildred Adair Stagg**

illustrated by Mary Lou Faltico

STANDARD
PUBLISHING

"As long as
the earth continues,
there will be
planting and harvest."

Genesis 8:21, 22
International
Children's Bible

A tiny plant is sleeping in the seed,
sleeping in the seed,
sleeping in the seed.
A tiny plant is sleeping in the seed,
showing God's great love.

The little seed is planted in the ground,
planted in the ground,
planted in the ground.
The little seed is planted in the ground,
showing God's great love.

The raindrops fall with a pitter, patter, pit,
pitter, patter, pit,
pitter, patter, pit.
The raindrops fall with a pitter, patter, pit,
showing God's great love.

The sun comes out to shine bright and warm,
shine bright and warm,
shine bright and warm.
The sun comes out to shine bright and warm,
showing God's great love.

The plant wakes up and stretches in the seed,
stretches in the seed,
stretches in the seed.

The plant wakes up and stretches in the seed,
showing God's great love.

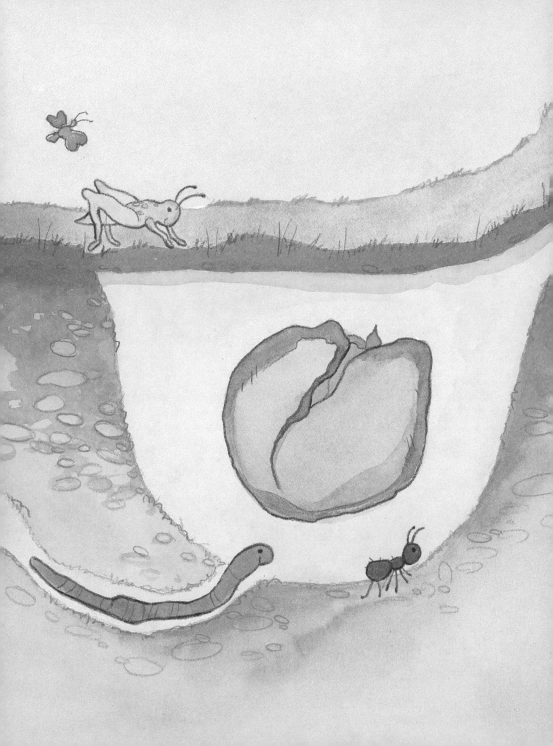

It humps its back and it opens with a pop!,
opens with a pop!,
opens with a pop!
It humps its back and it opens with a pop!,
showing God's great love.

The roots grow down, down, deep in the ground,
                            deep in the ground,
                            deep in the ground.
The roots grow down, down, deep in the ground,
showing God's great love.

The stem stands up and grows straight and tall,
grows straight and tall,
grows straight and tall.

The stem stands up and grows straight and tall,
showing God's great love.

Thank You, God, for seeds and rain and sun,
             seeds and rain and sun,
             seeds and rain and sun.
Thank You, God, for seeds and rain and sun,
showing us Your love.

For springtime always comes each year,
comes each year,
comes each year.
For springtime always comes each year,
showing us God's love.

Song of the Seed

CECILE LAMB

MILDRED ADAIR STAGG

A ti - ny plant is sleep-ing in the seed,

Sleep-ing in the seed, sleep-ing in the seed; A

ti - ny plant is sleep-ing in the seed, Show-ing God's great love.

Clap hands at the end of each verse
on the words "Showing God's great love."

The little seed is planted . . .

my plant is sleeping . . .

The raindrops fall . . .

The plant wakes up . . .

It humps its back . . .

the sun comes out . . .

the roots grow down . . .

The stem stands up . . .

Thank You, God, . . .